C000174740

The QE2 Story

The QE2 Story

Chris Frame and Rachelle Cross

The History Press

Published in the United Kingdom in 2009 by
The History Press
The Mill · Brimscombe Port · Stroud · Gloucestershire · GL5 2QG

British Library Cataloguing in Publication Data
A catalogue record for this book is available from the British Library.

Hardback ISBN 978-0-7524-5094-0

Half title page: QE2 *alongside in Piraeus, Greece. (Authors' Collection)*

Title page: QE2 *berthed in Sydney, Australia. (Authors' Collection)*

Typesetting and origination by The History Press
Printed in Italy

CONTENTS

ACKNOWLEDGEMENTS

We would like to thank everyone who helped us tell the *QE2*'s story. Special mentions go to Commodore Ronald W. Warwick for providing the photographic and historical material that made the writing of this book possible; Michael Gallagher from Cunard Line for providing historical information, photographs and reviewing the manuscript; Edda Zacharias, Wolfhard Scheer and Lloyd Werft Bremerhaven for providing photographs of *QE2*'s various refurbishments; Captain Ian McNaught and Chief Engineer Paul Yeoman for providing access to 'behind the scenes' areas aboard *QE2* as well as insight into the running of the ship, and Andrea Kaczmarek for keeping us up to date during *QE2*'s final voyages.

We are also extremely grateful to Amy Rigg, Emily Locke and the team at The History Press for all their ongoing hard work.

Thanks also to Andy Fitzsimmons, Carol Marlow, Colin Hargreaves, Gavin and Glennys Harper, Jan Frame, John Hargreaves, John Langley, Kenny Campbell, Mez Barter, Pam Massey, Renee Hewer, Rob Lightbody, Ron Burchett, Ross Burnside, Sam Warwick and Scott Becker for providing or assisting with the provision of material; Bill Miller for his ongoing encouragement; everyone at the *QE2* Story forum for 'keeping the legend alive'; and our families for supporting us.

Q*E2* is the most famous ship of our time. Beloved and cherished by legions of fans and the flagship of the British people, she was adored the world over, becoming an icon in many of the world's ports.

QE2 was built at a time when ocean liners were being retired en masse. The final roll of the dice for Cunard Line was to incorporate uniquely modern design elements into *QE2*, allowing her to take up winter residence in cruise ports around the world.

Since her launch in 1967, she endured to become the most travelled ship in history, covering over 6 million miles. She carried over 2.5 million passengers to more ports, on more voyages, than any ship before her.

On arrival in Dubai on 26 November 2008 her majestic ocean-going career came to an end. However, she did not slip away unnoticed. Her departure from Southampton on 11 November 2008 attracted hoards of Britons, all desperate to say one last goodbye to the ship they had known and loved for over forty years. Furthermore, she was given an

QE2 *arrives in Dubai, 26 November 2008. (Cunard Line)*

unforgettable welcome upon arrival at the Emirate that will direct her new career.

QE2's story is timeless – in decades to come people will still be talking about the one and only QE2. Her days as a Cunarder may have finally come to a close but the memories of those who have been touched by her live on.

◄ ◄
QE2 *passes by The Seven Sisters waterfall in Geiranger fjord. (Cunard Line)*

◄
QE2 *alongside in Piraeus. (Authors' Collection)*

◄
QE2's *distinctive funnel. (Authors' Collection)*

BACKGROUND

During her thirty-nine years of ocean-going service, *Queen Elizabeth 2* became the symbol of ocean liner travel. The saviour of her owners, the Cunard Line, *QE2*'s heritage dates back to 1839 when Sir Samuel Cunard travelled to England in an attempt to secure a British Government contract to provide a regular

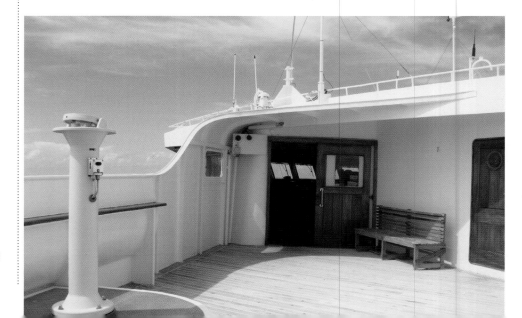

QE2*'s Bridge was the control centre for the ship. (Authors' Collection)*

➤➤

Queen Mary *docked at Southampton in 1963. (Colin Hargreaves)*

11

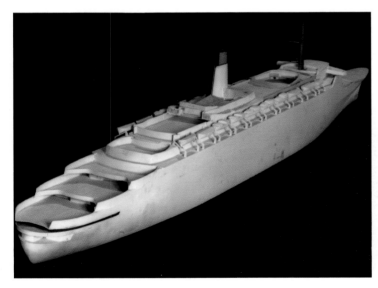

scheduled mail service across the North Atlantic Ocean.

Cunard, a savvy businessman, successfully won the mail contract, resulting in the formation of The British and North American Royal Mail Steam Packet Co., known – for simplicity's sake – as 'Cunard's Line'. With the backing of the Royal Mail contract Cunard was able to engage his entrepreneurial spirit, electing to include passenger accommodation in his new ships. Thus the age of scheduled transatlantic passenger crossings began.

During the creation of the new company, Cunard befriended legendary shipping architect Robert Napier. Napier had envisioned a transatlantic service for many years and eagerly assisted Cunard in the design of his new fleet.

Cunard's flagship the RMS *Britannia* was launched on 5 February 1840. Her maiden voyage departed from the English port of Liverpool on 4 July 1840. *Britannia* weighed 1,135 tons, was 207ft long and

Queen Mary *departing Southampton in 1963.* *(Colin Hargreaves)*

had a service speed of 9 knots. Upon her maiden arrival in Boston, Samuel Cunard was invited to no less than 1,873 dinner parties by delighted citizens of the American city.

The following decades saw Cunard Line grow in popularity, expand its services and reap ever greater profits, overcoming fierce competition at home and abroad in the form of the British White Star Line and the American Collin's Line. However, in the late 1800s the German lines proved to be Cunard's greatest threat. The liner *Kaiser Wilhelm der Grosse* captured the much coveted Blue Riband in 1897, to Britain's disgust.

By the early twentieth century, in a response to their German rivals, Cunard Line was planning the creation of two mammoth ships. At over 700ft long and with speeds of over 23.5 knots, the *Lusitania* and *Mauretania* were sure to recapture the Blue Riband for Britain, and with it restore British supremacy on the North Atlantic.

The two 'speed queens', as they became known, were joined in 1915 by the *Aquitania*. *Aquitania* (commonly referred to as 'Ship Beautiful') was larger and slightly slower than her sisters, but she was far more luxurious. With these three ships, Cunard Line was once again able to claim not only that they had the fastest fleet in the world but also the most lavish.

Mauretania and *Aquitania* were joined by the former German liner *Imperator* after the hostilities of the First World War. *Lusitania* had been lost to a German torpedo on 7 May 1915 – and *Imperator* was given to Cunard Line as war reparations. She was renamed *Berengaria* in 1920 and, despite her German heritage, became the flagship of the Cunard fleet.

Fifteen years later, Cunard's flagship was the legendary *Queen Mary*. Built at John Brown & Co. in Clydebank, she was joined during the Second World War by her larger sister, *Queen Elizabeth*.

The Queens served valiantly during the war, transporting both ANZAC and American troops to the war zone. To this day *Queen Mary* holds the record for the most people transported on an ocean liner in a single crossing – 16,082.

After the war the Queens became the very symbol of international travel. They were household names. Their speed (*Queen Mary* held the speed record for both westbound and eastbound crossings) as well as their sheer size (in excess of 80,000 tons and over 1,000ft apiece)

allowed Cunard Line to realise their long-held ambition of a two-ship, weekly transatlantic service. This resulted in a boom during the late 1940s and much of

Sir Samuel Cunard as depicted in QE2's *Mid-Ships Lobby.* (Authors' Collection)

the 1950s in what became known as the Golden Age of travel.

However, by the late 1950s all was not smooth sailing for Cunard Line. In fact, as early as 1957 it appeared as if the age of the ocean liner was coming to an end when, for the first time in history, more passengers 'crossed the pond' by air than by sea.

Cunard made various attempts to adapt to this new circumstance. Their fleet of ocean liners took on more and more pleasure cruises (for which they were totally unsuitable). The company also invested in a joint venture with BOAC to form BOAC-Cunard, a small subsidiary airline which undertook flights from Britain to the USA and the Tropics.

However, Cunard Line was at heart a shipping company, and the directors felt their future still lay in ships. So, during the dying days of the Atlantic passenger liner the company bet their fortunes and their future on a revolutionary new ocean liner, a ship they called Q4.

To be successful in the new environment where the jet aircraft dominated international travel routes, Cunard realised that their new ship needed to be designed with cruising in mind.

The first design for their next generation of ocean liner, codenamed Q3, was to be a 75,000-ton ship of similar dimensions to the old Queens. In essence, she was to be an updated version of the existing Queens – evolutionary rather than revolutionary. However, as the brief progressed the company realised that Q3 had fundamental flaws which caused much concern within the walls of the Cunard building in Liverpool.

Like the original Queens, her 1,000ft length meant Q3 would be unable to transit the Panama Canal (essential to global-cruising, unless the long passage

◄
The bulbous bow arrives at yard 736 awaiting installation. (Cunard Line)

'I name this ship *Queen Elizabeth the Second*'
HM Queen Elizabeth II at the launch of QE2.

17

➤
John Brown workers on the E-Stairway. (Cunard Line)

➤➤
Q4 Design Model from the forward angle showing the clutter-free foredeck. (Cunard Line)

⭕
Did you know?
QE2 was Cunard's
172nd ship.

around Cape Horn was to be made). Also, her deep draft would prevent her from entering the shallow ports of the Mediterranean and Caribbean.

On 19 October 1961 the plans for Q3 were permanently shelved. Cunard decided they could not justify building a new ship of such similar specification to the existing Queens. To make matters worse, the company was haemorrhaging money. Time was of the essence to find a replacement for the Q3 project.

Q4 was the codename given to Cunard's final hope. This new design was for a 55,000-ton, three-class liner with dimensions small enough to transit the locks of the Panama Canal. Her lightened weight was to be achieved by building her using a combination of steel and aluminium alloy, resulting in a shallower draft. Q4

Q4 Design Model from the aft angle showing the terraced Lido Decks. (Cunard Line)

could therefore undertake cruising to ports that the old Queens (and Q3) would have been unable to access.

The agreement on the dimensions of Q4 allowed Cunard to apply for assistance from the British Government, under the condition that the ship was built at a British yard. The application was accepted and a loan of £17.6 million was granted.

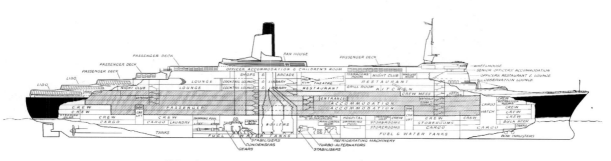

Q 4 — the new 58,000 ton CUNARDER

Q4 models were tested in water tanks simulating waves. (Cunard Line)

On 9 September 1964 the plans were sent to British yards that were willing to tender for the new ship. Cunard paid particular attention to the cost, construction timeline and handover date, announcing on 30 December 1964 that John Brown &

Co. of Clydebank had won the contract. The cost was set at £25,427,000, resulting in Cunard having to (despite their Government loan) mortgage eleven ships to raise the required funds.

2 July 1965 was selected as the date to lay the new ship's keel. She was to be built at the same berth as the earlier Queens and was given the yard number 736. However, when the time came to move the 180-ton keel into place, the yard's crane failed, resulting in it almost collapsing. Amid much embarrassment, the ceremony was abandoned and on 5 July 1965 an unceremonious keel laying was successfully completed.

736 was one of the first liners to be built with the aid of computers. However, despite this new technology, Cunard was keen to have a representative standing by the ship during her construction. As such, on 7 December 1966 the company announced Captain (later Commodore) William E. Warwick (relief captain to the old Queens) as Master Designate of the new Cunarder.

736 was revolutionary in many aspects. The ship's design employed some 1,100 tons

Cunard's iconic Liverpool headquarters forms part of Liverpool's 'Three Graces'. (Mez Barter)

of aluminium alloy in the superstructure – the most used on a ship at the time. The weight-saving aspects of this construction method allowed for a shallower draft, but also had the added bonus of increasing the ship's stability, which was further aided by the inclusion of four stabilisers. This allowed the restaurants and public rooms to be placed high in the superstructure. The shipyard also made use of pre-fabrication and built 736 as a welded hull (as opposed to using rivets).

The hull was made from steel and great care had to be taken when attaching the aluminium superstructure to the hull in order to avoid galvanic corrosion. An epoxy liquid was developed and applied to the joining surfaces to prevent the two metals from touching.

In July 1967 Cunard was faced by the daunting news that the new ship would most likely cost in the region of £28.5 million (more than £3 million over budget). This, coupled with the news that the existing fleet was set to lose a further £3.5 million, resulted in many sleepless nights for the company's management.

Did you know?

While smaller than *Queen Mary* and *Queen Elizabeth*, QE2 was still an impressive 963ft long.

In light of the increased building costs, Cunard appealed to the British Government for further assistance. HM Queen Elizabeth II had already agreed to name the new ship, and it was considered that any delay would cause much embarrassment for the company. However, of greater concern was the possibility of the Government opting to liquidate the unfinished liner, rather than risk losing more money. Fortunately, after two tense months, the Government agreed to increase the loan to £24 million, allowing work to continue.

On 20 September 1967 the Queen arrived at the shipyard in preparation for the launch of the new liner. Much consideration had been given to the name of the ship, which was publicly known only as 736. The name *Queen Elizabeth* was selected by Cunard Line – the elder Cunard Queen would be decommissioned by the time 736 entered service. However, this choice was kept in the strictest confidence, so much so that on the days leading up to the launch Glaswegian betting shops were taking wagers on the name of 736!

At the launch, the Queen was handed an envelope with the name inside. However, the envelope remained sealed as the Queen spoke into the microphone: 'I name this ship *Queen Elizabeth the Second* – may God bless her and all who sail in her.' Cunard later consulted Buckingham Palace regarding the name of the new ship, and it was agreed that the liner would be known as *Queen Elizabeth 2*, using the number 2 rather than the Roman numeral. *QE2* was born.

After her launch, *QE2* was moved to the fitting-out basin. John Brown & Co. had suffered significant financial losses during the construction of *QE2* and was no longer able to subsidise the shipyard. Thus, in January 1968, the John Brown Shipyard was absorbed into Upper Clyde Shipbuilders. The engine works was separated from the new company and remained John Brown Engineering.

Since the days of Q3, arguments had existed within Cunard as to whether the successor to the old Queens was to be a three- or two-class liner. *QE2* had originally been designed as a three-class ship, however, during the initial stages of her fitting-out, under the direction of Cunard's Chairman, Sir Basil Smallpeice, the design was altered to create a two-class layout.

'Ships have been boring long enough.'

Cunard's *QE2 marketing campaign – 1969.*

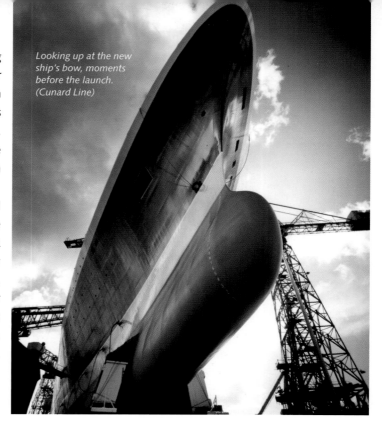

Looking up at the new ship's bow, moments before the launch. (Cunard Line)

This decision was made to emphasise *QE2*'s dual-purpose and, in particular, her role as a cruise ship.

The design team for *QE2*'s fit-out was led by Dan Wallace. Wallace had obtained vast amounts of information on successful interior designs from hotels and existing ocean liners and took this into careful consideration when designing *QE2*'s interior.

To be appealing in the competitive international travel market, *QE2* needed to offer passengers a great deal of creature comforts. Wallace took steps to ensure that *QE2*'s accommodation was top-class. The ship had a high percentage of outside cabins with large port-holes providing natural light. There was to be a greater number of inter-connecting rooms (for family cruising), fewer upper-bunks than

The Queen and The Duke of Edinburgh inspect the hull prior to the launch. (Cunard Line)

Ready for launch, Hull 736 towers over Clydebank. (Cunard Line)

Did you know?

1,100 tons of aluminium was used to build QE2's superstructure.

The 963ft-long hull enters its natural element for the first time. (Cunard Line)

The newly named QE2 makes her way into the Clyde. (Cunard Line)

Spectators watch as QE2 *enters the water. (Courtesy of R.W. Warwick;* QE2 – The Cunard Line Flagship Queen Elizabeth 2*)*

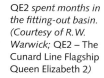

QE2 *spent months in the fitting-out basin. (Courtesy of R.W. Warwick;* QE2 – The Cunard Line Flagship Queen Elizabeth 2*)*

Safely launched, QE2 *rests in the River Clyde. (Courtesy of R.W. Warwick;* QE2 – The Cunard Line Flagship Queen Elizabeth 2*)*

lounge. She was also given four swimming pools (two indoors for use on the Atlantic) and large amounts of open deck space for sun-worshippers. The end result was a ship quite unlike the old Cunard fleet. In fact, so sure were Cunard that QE2 would change the face of ocean travel, they launched a marketing campaign for her stating that 'Ships have been boring long enough'.

QE2 was one of the fastest passenger ships ever built. Her original steam turbine power plant was designed and built by John Brown Engineering. It consisted of three boilers which produced super-heated steam for the turbines. This generated 110,000 shaft horsepower. The electrical generators within QE2 created enough power to supply a town of 20,000 people.

It had been Cunard's desire to have QE2 completed on schedule, but even before

seen on the previous Queens and private bathroom facilities for each of QE2's cabins.

QE2's design also included numerous public rooms. There were nightclubs, a piano bar, a two-level theatre, two ballrooms, a card room, two libraries and an observation

◄◄
The ship nears completion – note the lack of Bridge Wings and mast. (Courtesy of R.W. Warwick; QE2 – The Cunard Line Flagship Queen Elizabeth 2)

◄
QE2's mast is carefully hoisted aboard. (Cunard Line)

the ship's launch it was clear that she would not be ready in time for the proposed spring-summer season of 1968. The revised plan was to have *QE2* ready by December 1968. However, constant industrial action and vandalism aboard meant that this date was also pushed back.

After Upper Clyde Shipbuilders took control of the completion of *QE2*, Cunard worked very closely with them in an attempt to speed up the ship's readiness for sea. She was now considerably behind schedule, which had daunting ramifications for Cunard's bottom line.

The new ship was due to undertake a series of trials in late 1968 which would keep her at sea for the equivalent time of a round-trip transatlantic crossing. *QE2* would also need to spend time in both hot and cold weather so her air-conditioning could be tested.

Cunard were aware that the trials would undoubtedly result in a series of amendments and alterations to the machinery, and as such, adjusted their expectations, predicting that the *QE2* would enter service in January 1969.

In order for work to be completed, *QE2* had to make the short journey to Greenock. Both Cunard and Upper Clyde Shipbuilders were extremely relieved when, on 19 November 1968, the new ship made her way down the Clyde for the first time. So significant was this event that Western Scotland declared a public holiday to allow citizens to witness the magnificent new Queen make her very first voyage. To mark the occasion, Prince Charles joined Captain William E. Warwick on the Bridge. *QE2* departed Clydebank with a whistle blast given by the prince.

Once at Greenock, work on *QE2* was slowed by ongoing industrial disputes. There was also an epidemic of looting aboard the ship. The ship's workforce was well aware that *QE2* could be one of their

QE2 *powers through final acceptance trials. (Cunard Line)*

Did you know?
QE2's keel was originally to be laid on 2 July 1965, but it proved so heavy the cranes broke!

35

▶
QE2 *at speed during basin trials. (Cunard Line)*

▶▶
QE2*'s beauty is evident in this early shot of her in her original configuration. (Cunard Line)*

final contracts – such was the shambles of the British shipbuilding industry at this time. In an attempt to secure their short-term finances, several members of the workforce took to removing valuable items from the unfinished ship. Black market sales fetched high prices for goods such as copper piping, carpeting and furniture.

Despite the ongoing issues with her internal fit-out, *QE2*'s sea trials commenced on 26 November 1968. The trials initially appeared to be very successful, with the ship building up speed to an impressive 29.5 knots.

The trials came to an abrupt halt when an oil leak into the high-pressure steam system was identified. There was no choice but to return to dry-dock where the entire steam-turbine system was thoroughly cleaned out. The delay resulted in the cancellation of a planned Christmas charity cruise, causing Cunard further frustrations.

When the sea trials recommenced the ship achieved an outstanding 32.46 knots, and arrangements were quickly made to commence the ship's final acceptance trials.

➤
Commodore William E. Warwick, HM Queen Elizabeth II, and Cunard Chairman Sir Basil Smallpeice inspect the new Cunard flagship. (Courtesy of R.W. Warwick; QE2 – The Cunard Line Flagship Queen Elizabeth 2*)*

These began on 23 December 1968 with 500 members of Cunard's staff and their families as guests. However, much of the passenger accommodation was unfinished and in need of cleaning, resulting in the 'guests' having to work for their passage. In addition to the 500 Cunard families that were hard at work, 200 members of the fitting-out crew were busy putting the finishing touches to the ship's interior.

The acceptance trials were interrupted when both the starboard and port high-pressure turbines malfunctioned (it was later discovered that the turbine blades had shattered, causing catastrophic failure of the propulsion system). QE2 sailed slowly to Southampton on a wave of bad publicity. On 29 December 1968, in light of the as yet undetermined cause of the turbine failure and the state of disarray within the public rooms, Cunard cancelled all future sailings and issued the following statement:

> Cunard can not accept delivery until after the ship's turbines have been thoroughly re-tested and proved in further basin trials and speed trials and a prolonged acceptance trial under maintained pressure, followed by further inspection. It is impossible to say when this programme of correction, testing and proving of the ship's power can be completed.

This statement had the desired effect of motivating Upper Clyde Shipbuilders to increase their efforts in identifying and resolving the turbine issue, and to have QE2's interiors completed by the time of the ship's maiden voyage. Over the following two months the turbines were repaired

Did you know?
QE2 was fifteen minutes late leaving on her maiden voyage.

Commodore William E. Warwick, Prince Charles and Cunard Chairman Sir Basil Smallpeice, during QE2's first voyage. (Cunard Line)

and thoroughly tested, and, to Cunard's great relief, this time they performed to specification.

Finally, on 18 April 1969, *QE2* was officially accepted by Cunard Line at a total cost of £29,091,000. The ship departed on a mini-maiden voyage to the Canary Islands on 22 April and, upon her return, was provisioned and made ready for her first transatlantic crossing.

On the eve of this momentous voyage, the ship was inspected by HM Queen Elizabeth II and Prince Phillip. Captain William Warwick proudly escorted the Queen and Duke of Edinburgh around his beautiful new command. This tour started what was a long and successful career for *QE2*.

Did you know?
QE2 had a welded hull. As a result very few rivets were used.

EARLY LIFE

QE2's very stylish mast.
(Cunard Line)

The flagship of the British Merchant Navy arrives in New York at the culmination of her maiden voyage. (Courtesy of R.W. Warwick; QE2 – The Cunard Line Flagship Queen Elizabeth 2)

QE2's first Atlantic crossing was completed in four days, sixteen hours and thirty-five minutes, at an average speed of just over 28 knots. After so much anticipation, her arrival in New York Harbour was spectacular. She was greeted by a coastguard ship and a Navy destroyer, as well as a flotilla of smaller pleasure craft.

 The Double Down Room was QE2's Tourist Class Lounge. (Cunard Line)

 The Lookout Bar was located on the forward end of Upper Deck. (Cunard Line)

Unlike the earlier Queens, QE2 had a single mast. (Cunard Line)

QE2's original funnel was a vast departure from traditional Cunard. (Cunard Line)

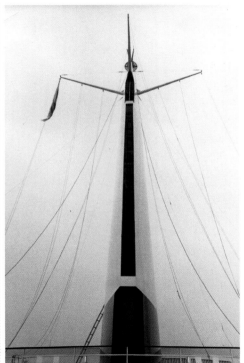

One thousand guests were invited to a party on board the Queen to celebrate.

Cunard were delighted with the popularity of their new ship. *QE2*'s voyages were so well booked that by October of 1969 Cunard was able to repay £2.5 million of their Government loan, and set up a plan to repay £500,000 every six months thereafter. Her first winter season involved a series of ten-day cruises to the Caribbean, allowing for a number of spectacular maiden arrivals in the Caribbean ports. These cruises proved very popular and showcased the advantages of her dual-purpose design.

It was whilst anchored off the port of Castries in Saint Lucia on 8 January 1971 that *QE2*'s radio room received a distress call from the stricken French liner *Antilles*. The 19,828-ton ship had run aground and caught fire off the coast of Mustique in the Grenadines. *QE2* was already preparing to sail so was able to respond quickly. Within three and a half hours the *QE2* had reached the burning liner and was able to take the 500 survivors who had been evacuated to the islands of Mustique and Bequia aboard. There was no loss of life but the *Antilles* was unable to be saved, despite the determined efforts of her captain and officers.

Sadly, in spite of *QE2*'s popularity, soaring fuel costs (increases of over 80 per cent) and an economic recession in the United States resulted in Cunard posting a loss of £1.9 million for the year 1970. Although 1971 was forecast to show increases in cruise bookings of 10 per cent on the previous year, the industry was being hindered by a US Government advertising campaign

Did you know?
Prince Charles was *QE2*'s first official passenger.

The beautiful Queen Elizabeth 2 *in her role as a cruise ship. (Cunard Line)*

aimed at encouraging Americans to stay at home.

Despite this downturn in fortunes, Cunard's share price was rising on the London Stock Exchange. Rumours begun to circulate that the 132-year-old company would be sold. These rumours came to fruition when, in August 1971, Cunard Line was bought by Trafalgar House Co. for £27.3 million.

Public attention turned immediately to the future of *QE2*. However, Trafalgar House quickly defused the situation by announcing that Cunard would remain a shipping company within the Trafalgar Group, and that *QE2* would continue to operate as a British-flagged liner.

During the first six months of Trafalgar House ownership a total survey was undertaken of *QE2* and the services that

The Queens Room in its original design was the First Class Lounge. (Cunard Line)

Did you know?
QE2 undertook twenty-six world cruises during her service career.

were offered aboard the ship. This resulted in £1 million being spent on upgrades to the ship, which included the addition of balcony penthouse accommodation to Signal and Sun Deck. The work was completed whilst the ship was in Southampton.

17 May 1972 saw QE2 face a new threat when, two days into an eastbound transatlantic crossing, the ship received a coded telegraph message from the New York office. The message stated that an anonymous caller had threatened to detonate explosive devices on QE2 during the crossing unless a US$350,000 ransom was paid.

The crew, under the command of Captain William Law, were organised to undertake a security sweep of the ship, which proved fruitless. A professional bomb disposal unit was also engaged to do their own search in order to confirm the ship's safety. The RAF sent a four-man team who were parachuted into the sea and picked up by two of QE2's boats.

As the passengers enjoyed an evening's entertainment, the bomb disposal unit

The Columbia Restaurant located on Quarter Deck. This room later became Mauretania Restaurant and then again changed to Caronia Restaurant. (Cunard Line)

conducted another search of the ship, but again nothing was found. The ship continued on its way to Cherbourg and Southampton without further incident. The perpetrator was eventually caught when making similar threats to American Airlines

'Ladies and Gentlemen, we have received information concerning a threat of a bomb-explosion on board this ship some time during this voyage. We have received such threats in the past, which have so far turned out to be hoaxes. However, we always take them seriously and take every possible precaution.
On this occasion we are being assisted by the British Government who are sending out bomb disposal experts who will be parachuted into the sea and picked up by boat and brought aboard.
I will of course keep you fully informed about the situation. Cunard are taking every precaution ashore and on board and will take any necessary action to minimise risk. If there is any question of it being necessary to pay over money, this will be done ashore in New York.
I can only ask you to remain calm. On these occasions lots of rumours tend to circulate. Please only take notice of any information that comes from me directly or from one of my officers. That is all for the moment.'

Captain William Law – Announcement when bomb threat was made to QE2 in 1972.

and was sentenced to prison for twenty years.

The *QE2* faced further drama in 1973 when she was chartered by Assured Travel of Worcester to transport Jewish pilgrims from Southampton to Israel for the country's twenty-fifth anniversary. Due to the state of affairs in the area at this time, there was a fear of attack resulting in the crew demanding danger money for the voyage. The round-trip voyage was completed without incident; however, it later became known that President Anwar Sadat of Egypt had personally countermanded an order to torpedo *QE2*.

In a BBC interview given by President Sadat in 1974, he explained that Colonel Gadaffi of Libya, who at the time was sharing arms with Egypt, had ordered an Egyptian submarine to sink the *QE2* in

retaliation for the loss of a Libyan airliner shot down by Israel in 1972. The submarine captain could have carried out the order but, fortunately for *QE2*, he sought to first confirm his orders with the Egyptian President.

Balcony Accommodation is craned aboard in Southampton. (Courtesy of R. W. Warwick; QE2 – The Cunard Line Flagship Queen Elizabeth 2*)*

FOR QUEEN AND COUNTRY

The Falklands War in 1982 would prove to be a turning point in *QE2*'s career. The officers and crew heard on BBC Radio 2 on 3 May that their ship had been requisitioned by the Government. This news was officially confirmed, and Captain Alexander Hutcheson made the formal announcement that the ship would be withdrawn from commercial service upon return to Southampton.

Work to make the ship ready for war began as soon as she arrived home. This included cutting off the aft decks to create two large helipads on Quarter and One Deck, in the space normally occupied by two of the ship's swimming pools. This area had already been reinforced to hold the weight of the water in the pools and, as such, was easily convertible to hold the weight of helicopters.

Other work involved protecting the interiors. Pictures, furniture and plants were removed and stored in warehouses ashore and the carpets were covered with sheets of hardboard. The Double Down Room (later to become the Grand Lounge) was converted into a mess for the soldiers. Military stores and equipment were brought aboard by the ton.

On 12 May, after eight days of extensive conversion work, the ship was ready to embark 3,000 men (from the Fifth Infantry Brigade, including the Scots Guards, Welsh Guards and the Gurkhas), who boarded to the sound of pipes. *QE2* set sail that afternoon, bound for the South Atlantic. Due to the danger that *QE2* would be subject to on her passage, it was decided that the ship would spend as little time as possible in hostile waters, and

considerations were made to allow *QE2* to refuel at sea. This risky operation had never been undertaken aboard *QE2* before and, as such, during her transit of the Channel, the Royal Fleet Auxiliary vessel *Grey Rover* rendezvoused with the Cunard flagship to practice the manoeuvre.

QE2 sailed south with a small fleet of Sea King helicopters aboard, which had taken up residence on her aft helipads. The helicopters formed part of the new routine aboard the ship. Flight training, exercise

◄◄
QE2's aft decks were cut away to make room for Sea King helicopters. (Courtesy of R.W. Warwick; QE2 – The Cunard Line Flagship Queen Elizabeth 2)

◄
QE2 rendezvouses with Grey Rover to practice refuelling-at-sea. (Courtesy of R.W. Warwick; QE2 – The Cunard Line Flagship Queen Elizabeth 2)

drills and firing practice were undertaken on a regular basis to ensure the men were ready for combat.

On 18 May *QE2* diverted to Freetown Harbour in Sierra Leone to refuel. Security around the ship was so tight that *QE2* managed to depart the West African port without being noticed by the world's press.

The ship then proceeded south to Ascension Island where she was replenished with 200 tons of stores. During the passage to the island, the crew busied themselves creating a 'blackout' environment on board, covering every window and porthole with black plastic.

After departing Ascension Island the vessel operated under electronic silence. The radar was turned off, leaving the officers to rely on traditional navigation techniques. Military lookouts were placed around the ship and the water-tight doors were closed in anticipation of possible attack.

Shortly after 7:20 p.m. on 27 May, *QE2* arrived at her planned rendezvous point in Cumberland Bay. There she met other British vessels including the P&O liner *Canberra*. That evening, troops begun to be transferred from *QE2* to

Canberra and *Norland* via helicopters and the ship's launches, as well as the admiralty tug *Typhoon*. By nightfall the operation was all but over, and *QE2*'s Sea King helicopters took up residency aboard *Canberra*.

On 29 May *QE2* took on survivors from the HMS *Ardent*, HMS *Coventry* and HMS *Antelope*. News of the attack on the British tanker *British Wye*, 400 miles north of *QE2*'s position, made the danger for the ship extremely apparent. Further concern resulted from reports that the Argentinean Air Force had used a Boeing 707 in an attempt to locate *QE2* during her journey south. It was decided that *QE2* should not be in the danger zone for any longer than was absolutely necessary, and the ship departed just before 5:30 p.m.

Severe weather conditions meant that the ship could not refuel for the first two days of her passage, and the ship's supplies became alarmingly low. On 2 June the fuel reserve dropped to less than 1,000 tons, forcing the refuelling operation to be attempted despite the weather conditions. *QE2* met with the Royal Fleet auxiliary vessel *Bayleaf* and successfully took over

Target practice replaced Afternoon Tea as one of the most important daily rituals during QE2's Falklands Service. (Courtesy of R. W. Warwick; QE2 – The Cunard Line Flagship Queen Elizabeth 2)

Landing a Sea King helicopter on a moving ship was a risky business! (Courtesy of R.W. Warwick; QE2 – The Cunard Line Flagship Queen Elizabeth 2)

Snow on the bow as the ship sailed south. (Courtesy of R.W. Warwick; QE2 – The Cunard Line Flagship Queen Elizabeth 2)

3,800 tons of fuel, allowing her to sustain 25 knots for the remainder of her journey home.

QE2 entered the Solent at 9:00 a.m. on 11 June 1982. She was met by Admiral Sir John Fieldhouse, Commander-in-Chief of the Royal Navy, and Lord Matthews who arrived aboard by helicopter to address the survivors. QE2 was then joined by the

Royal Yacht *Britannia* with HM Queen Elizabeth the Queen Mother waving at the hundreds of people lining the decks of the giant Cunard liner. The Queen Mother then sent a message to Captain Jackson which read:

> I am pleased to welcome you back as *QE2* returns to home waters after your tour of duty in the South Atlantic. The exploits of your own ship's company and the deeds of valour of those who served in *Antelope*, *Coventry* and *Ardent* have been acclaimed throughout the land and I am proud to add my personal tribute.

So ended *QE2*'s military career, during which she had steamed 14,967 miles in less than thirty days. She was now ready for a well-deserved rest and refurbishment.

REPLACEMENT OR REBIRTH?

After returning from service in the South Atlantic, QE2 was treated to the Government-funded refurbishment which had been promised to Cunard in exchange for using their flagship in military service. The refit's sole aim was to return the ship to her pre-war glory. However, Cunard took this opportunity to make some significant alterations to QE2.

One of the most talked about internal changes was the rebuilding of the Six Deck swimming pool (located off the F Stairway) to create the Golden Door Spa-at-Sea, based on an expensive and exclusive wellness spa of the same name on land. This complimentary extra delighted QE2 passengers, so much so that similar additions were made aboard Sagafjord and Vistafjord.

The Queens Grill was redecorated by Dennis Lennon (who had worked on the ship's original designs) and QE2's interior was refreshed with 27km of new carpet. This time out of service was also used to begin a series of alterations to the aft-end

QE2 passes the Statue of Liberty prior to her 1896/87 re-engine. (Cunard Line)

of Quarter Deck, which would eventually house the Lido.

QE2 appeared from the refit refreshed, sporting a new livery of pebble-grey hull with traditional Cunard colours upon her once white-and-black funnel. While traditionalists welcomed the change to *QE2*'s funnel, the general public did not warm to the ship's new, lighter hull colour, which also proved difficult to maintain. After several months it was decided to return the hull to its original colours.

In 1983, the remaining work to the Lido was completed when, in Bremerhaven, a Magrodome was fitted over the Quarter Deck pool. The addition of the Magrodome (a sliding glass roof) allowed the area to be used during inclement weather, and thus the Lido seating could spill out into the area which was once an open deck.

QE2 *at speed – her new funnel giving her a far more commanding profile. (Cunard Line)*

Did you know?
QE2 was Cunard's longest serving flagship.

During the 1980s *QE2*'s engines became increasingly unreliable causing several highly publicised breakdowns. As a result, Cunard investigated options for the future of *QE2*, including the building of a replacement vessel. However, it was estimated that re-engining the *QE2* would be far cheaper than building a new ship, and in 1983 shipyards around the world were invited to tender for the work.

The contract to undertake the work was awarded to Lloyd Werft Shipyard in Bremerhaven, Germany. There, *QE2* was fitted with a diesel electric plant – the first of its kind on a passenger vessel.

QE2's final steam-powered transatlantic crossing departed from New York on 20 October 1986. This crossing was a significant one in the 147-year history of Cunard Line as it would also signal the

QE2's forward diesel engine room in its final configuration. (Authors' Collection)

The Club Lido and Quarter Deck Pool with the Magrodome closed above. (Cunard Line)

QE2's new funnel was a welcome addition to the ship. (Authors' Collection)

One of nine massive diesel engines. (Courtesy of R.W. Warwick; QE2 – The Cunard Line Flagship Queen Elizabeth 2)

The original starboard propeller shaft is removed. (Courtesy of R.W. Warwick; QE2 – The Cunard Line Flagship Queen Elizabeth 2)

end of the Cunard steamship era. By the end of *QE2*'s life as a steamship she had sailed 2,622,858 nautical miles in just under eighteen years.

The ship arrived in Bremerhaven on 27 October 1986, and work begun immediately on the mammoth refurbishment programme. To facilitate the removal of the original steam power plant the funnel was removed and stored on the dockside. This allowed for a crane to winch the old engines and associated machinery out through the casing.

During the refit some 4,700 tons of metal (which made up the steam plant) were removed from *QE2*. In its place, nine medium-speed MAN B&W engines were lowered into place, each weighing an impressive 220 tons. *QE2*'s diesel engines had an individual output of 10,620kw (or

The first diesel engine is in place. (Courtesy of Wolfhard Scheer)

65

Bracing is installed to hold the new funnel. (Courtesy of Wolfhard Scheer)

Did you know?

QE2 was named after the first (Cunard) Queen Elizabeth and not the reigning monarch.

◄
The modified, wider funnel is craned aboard. (Courtesy of Wolfhard Scheer)

Positioning the funnel was a tricky manoeuvre. (Courtesy of Wolfhard Scheer)

Did you know?
QE2's original funnel was removed during her 1986/87 refurbishment.

*Finally, QE2 looks
like a Cunarder again.
(Courtesy of Wolfhard
Scheer)*

14,242hp) at 400rpm. The diesel engines were arranged in two groups – four in the forward engine room and five in the aft. However, the diesel engines did not directly move *QE2*. Instead they were connected via a flexible coupling to an alternator, which allowed them to produce electricity.

From here, power was directed to various areas of the ship, including those devoted to providing hotel services. Power was also fed into two propulsion motors. These motors were built by GEC Large Machines Ltd, England, and weighed 295 tons each. Running at 144rpm and rated at 44mw, they were the largest single-unit propulsion motors to have been incorporated into a commercial vessel at the time.

The propulsion motors were each connected to a 230ft-long propeller shaft which allowed them to drive the ship's new variable-pitch propellers. *QE2* was given two five-bladed propellers, each 22ft in diameter. Their design allowed greater flexibility and manoeuvrability as the propeller shaft always remained in operation at 144rpm (reduced to 72rpm when entering ports via 11mw converters)

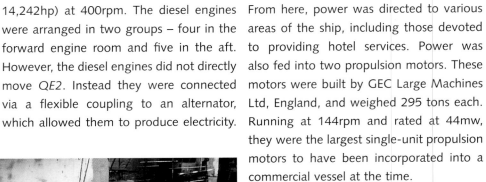

QE2's new port propeller shaft is installed. (Courtesy of R.W. Warwick; QE2 – The Cunard Line Flagship Queen Elizabeth 2)

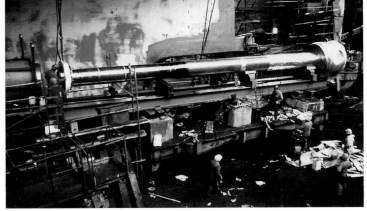

with speed and direction being controlled by the pitch of the propeller blades.

With the new engines in place, a new funnel was fitted to the ship. Incorporating much of the original cowling, the new funnel was wider to accommodate the nine diesel exhaust pipes.

The time spent in dry-dock was also used to undertake an internal refurbishment. This work included the creation of the Mauretania Restaurant in the space previously occupied by the Tables of the World Restaurant, and the completion of penthouse suites on Signal Deck which, along with the reworked funnel, gave QE2 a new, more powerful profile.

Upon completion of the engine conversion the ship began a series of sea trials, which produced pleasing results, with a top speed of almost 34 knots. The ship was not only faster and more economical than before, but vibration levels were also curtailed as a result of the diesel engines being secured on top of anti-vibration mountings. During the sea trials interior work was continued, having, again, run over schedule.

QE2's steam turbine engines are inspected for their scrap value. (Courtesy of R.W. Warwick; QE2 – The Cunard Line Flagship Queen Elizabeth 2)

Did you know?
QE2 had nine diesel
electric engines, each
the size of a London
double-decker bus!

The revitalised (albeit incomplete) QE2
was handed over to Cunard on 25 April
1987. This signalled the completion of the
mammoth marine conversion which had
taken an incredible 1.7 million man hours
to complete.

QE2 returned to service on 29 April 1987
with a special commemorative voyage
down the Solent, from Southampton to
an anchorage just off the Isle of Wight.
She was joined by HRH Diana, Princess
of Wales, who met QE2 aboard a launch.
The Princess was travelling with a group of
underprivileged children from Southampton
who were entertained aboard QE2 as she
made the return trip.

Upon arrival in Southampton, the crew
busied themselves preparing the ship for her
'Second Maiden Voyage'. During her time
in Bremerhaven many of QE2's experienced
British crew left after being offered the
choice between becoming a contracted
employee or being given a redundancy
package. The replacement crew members

were unfamiliar with the ship which, along with the incomplete state of many of her public rooms, resulted in a less than perfect experience for guests.

Despite the on-board problems, *QE2* returned to New York after completing her first diesel-powered transatlantic crossing. There she was given a jubilant welcome from her 'second home'. The Queen gradually settled back into a smooth schedule of crossings and cruises, and once again delighted guests with her charm and character.

QE2's elegant lines were timeless. (Authors' Collection)

THE NEW *QE2*

Project Lifestyle achieved the goal of continuity and flow between public rooms. (Authors' Collection)

The Japanese people adored *QE2*, and this was no more evident than in 1989 when she was chartered twice. The first occasion was in March when a consortium of Japanese businessmen chartered the ship for seventy-two days to celebrate the 130th anniversary of Yokohama.

The ship was used as a hotel and entertainment precinct whilst docked at the passenger terminal. Visitors were free to shop at the International Shopping Concourse (later the Royal Promenade) and eat at the on-board restaurants during the day. Guests also came aboard to spend the night.

Did you know?

QE2 was 4,464 gross-registered-tons larger when retired than she was when placed into service.

> Cunard's 'go faster' speed stripe and Golden Lion decals on the ship's superstructure. (Authors' Collection)

> Looking up at QE2's Boat Deck during a 1998 cruise. (Authors' Collection)

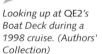

< Sporting a new livery of Royal Blue hull with Speed Stripe, QE2 is seen in Auckland, 1995. (Authors' Collection)

QE2's Grand Lounge was given a totally new look during 'Project Lifestyle'. (Cunard Line)

The Mauretania Restaurant briefly occupied the Quarter Deck restaurant space before reverting to the Caronia Restaurant. (Cunard Line)

Cunard's flagship seen here at speed in an otherwise still ocean. (Cunard Line)

In December of that year *QE2* returned to Japan for a further six-month charter, this time in Osaka, which coincided with the World Exposition. After the charter, *QE2* was able to undertake a series of cruises in the Western Pacific and South China Sea.

Art deco-style units replaced original bathroom fittings. (Authors' Collection)

The Mauretania Restaurant entrance in 1998. (Authors' Collection)

A painting of Princess Elizabeth and Prince Phillip formed part of the Heritage Trail. (Authors' Collection)

Did you know?

Four Deck had a lower ceiling than any other passenger deck.

Upon her return to transatlantic service, *QE2* made her fastest eastbound crossing, achieving an average speed of over 30 knots. The journey, under the command of Captain Robin Woodall, took four days, six hours and fifty-seven minutes.

Cunard Line celebrated its 150th anniversary in 1990. The *QE2* undertook a number of celebratory cruises, which involved several maiden calls, including her first call to Ireland (Cóbh – formerly Queenstown – famous for being the last port of call for *Titanic*), her first call to Scotland since her construction and a maiden call to Liverpool (where it was estimated over a million people turned out to see her).

Although *QE2* has often been involved in celebrations, she has also suffered from the occasional bout of embarrassment. One such occasion occurred in August 1992 when undertaking a cruise past Martha's Vineyard, bound for New York. During this particular voyage the ship was sailing south of Cuttyhunk Island under control of

'It was the grandest of days; Cunard was celebrating 150 wonderful years in July 1990. Aboard the *Vistafjord* as we waited off Portsmouth for the arrival of Her Majesty the Queen on-board the *Britannia*, the centrepiece of the occasion was, however, the ever-glorious *QE2*. She was moored in centre position. Topped by her proud orange-red and black funnel, she looked the absolute epitome of a classic ocean liner, of Cunard itself, of transatlantic history. Indeed, no ship in recent years has had more majesty than the *QE2*.'

Bill Miller, maritime historian.

Did you know?
QE2 was the fastest merchant ship at the time of her retirement.

QE2's Magrodome was removed in the 1994 refit. (Courtesy of R.W. Warwick; QE2 – The Cunard Line Flagship Queen Elizabeth 2)

Did you know?

QE2 had twenty-five masters during her career.

a pilot when suddenly those on the Bridge experienced a series of sharp vibrations and a rumbling sound. Captain Woodall, anticipating that the ship may have struck something, ordered the telegraph set to 'all stop' and the crew mustered to emergency stations whilst the vessel was checked for possible damage.

It was discovered that the ship had indeed struck uncharted ridges on the southern tip of Sow and Pigs Reef (it was later found that the charts of the area had not been updated for fifty years, and showed the depth of the water as being far greater than it actually was). Water was found in several compartments of *QE2*'s double-bottom, which caused understandable concern. However, calculations showed that *QE2*'s stability would remain within safe parameters. Nevertheless, the US Coastguard was informed and the ship was ordered to anchor nearby and await inspection for possible oil pollution. Further formalities ensued, including the captain, first officer and pilot being tested for drug and alcohol consumption.

The following day the ship was granted permission to make way to Newport where the passengers were disembarked. *QE2* was then able to proceed to Boston where repairs were to be undertaken. Unfortunately, upon dry-docking and inspection, the damage was found to be far more severe than originally anticipated. The shipyard was unable to make full repairs as they did not have the resources (or the correct grade of steel) to do so. As such, they made temporary repairs to *QE2*'s hull before the ship sailed to Blohm + Voss Shipyard in Hamburg where permanent repairs were completed.

During the early 1990s much debate occurred within the hierarchy of Cunard management as to the future of *QE2*. Twenty years of refurbishment had resulted in *QE2*'s interior becoming somewhat disjointed. Themes ranged from 1960s retro to classic art deco, with a sprinkling of 1980s flair. Therefore, a massive rebuild of *QE2*'s interior was required in order to ensure

Did you know?
The Grill Room (later Princess Grill) was originally *QE2*'s most exclusive restaurant.

that the Cunard flagship could survive the 1990s to sail on into the twenty-first century. 'Project Lifestyle' was to provide QE2 with a new lease of life. An impressive £45 million was budgeted to create what Cunard dubbed the 'New QE2'.

Cunard entrusted the British MET Studio to oversee the ship's transformation, and Blohm + Voss Shipyard was again selected to undertake the work. This project would see the redesign of nearly every major public room as well as the refurbishment of all passenger accommodation. Even more ambitious was the company's decision to rebuild every bathroom aboard QE2, replacing the original fixtures and fittings with art deco-styled units.

A thirty-two-day schedule was allocated to the most ambitious interior refit project QE2 would ever undertake. This short timeframe put considerable strain on the shipyard, with a workforce of 2,000 people (plus 400 QE2 crew) working around the clock in an attempt to complete the job on time.

One of the most welcome changes included the removal of QE2's Magrodome and Quarter Deck swimming pool to make way for an enhanced Lido. As novel as the Magrodome was, it proved impractical, causing a greenhouse effect when closed. Its removal allowed for the addition of 5,000 sq. ft of open deck space aft of the enlarged Yacht Club.

The ship was also given a new exterior identity, including a Royal Blue hull and the addition of a tricolour 'speed stripe' along the superstructure between Quarter and One Deck. These colours formed the new Cunard livery and received a mixed reception.

Did you know?

QE2 was 68ft shorter than her namesake, RMS *Queen Elizabeth*.

Further on-board enhancements included the addition of the Cunard Heritage Trail. This saw pieces of Cunard history scattered about *QE2* in the form of a guided (or self-guided) walking tour.

Sadly, the short timescale given for the refit proved insufficient to complete the work, resulting in the ship sailing for Southampton unfinished. Upon arrival in Southampton, the marine safety office inspected the vessel and, due to the incomplete state of the ship's accommodation, restricted *QE2*'s passenger certificate to 1,000 passengers including workmen. Around 460 passengers were informed that they couldn't sail aboard the ship's scheduled transatlantic crossing, resulting in the company having to give full refunds (and the promise of a future free cruise) to all affected.

Those passengers who did sail sent mixed messages to family and friends ashore. The press became involved and upon arrival in New York the ship was met by the Coastguard who issued a Certificate of Control Verification for a Foreign Vessel.

The resulting negative media coverage left *QE2*'s reputation tarnished. It was not until her 1995 World Cruise, when the public saw the results achieved during the 1994 refit, that she regained her place in the public mind as the 'Queen of the Seas'.

Did you know?
QE2's signal letters were G.B.T.T. – the same letters used for RMS *Queen Mary* until her retirement in 1967.

THE GOLDEN YEARS

➤

QE2 alongside during a call at Melbourne. (Authors' Collection)

Did you know?

When *QE2* transited the locks of the Panama Canal there was only 5ft to spare.

The sheer strength of *QE2* was tested during a westbound transatlantic crossing in September 1995. During this particular voyage the ship encountered rough seas due to her proximity to Hurricane Luis. On 11 September at 2:10 a.m. the captain and officers on the Bridge sighted a huge wave with an estimated height of 95ft. Less than a minute later the wave crashed across the bow of *QE2*, clearing the Bridge. Several bow plates and some of the railings were dented by the weight of the water, but the ship escaped largely unscathed.

QE2's encounter with Hurricane Luis could have been considered a precursor to the rough weather ahead for Cunard Line. 1996 saw The Trafalgar House Co. being acquired by Kvaerner for £904 million. This sale, by default, included the Cunard Line which was not a major focus for Kvaerner.

As a result, money was not freely available for investment in Cunard's fleet, leading to standards slipping. Furthermore, at a time when other lines were increasing their new tonnage, the Cunard fleet was ageing, with no new builds since *Cunard Princess* in 1977.

The following eighteen months saw several key changes in the Cunard fleet, with the departure of the four-star fleet consisting of *Cunard Countess*, *Cunard Princess*, *Cunard Crown Dynasty* and *Cunard Crown Jewel*. *Sagafjord* was also sold, and became the *Saga Ruby* for Saga Cruises.

Kvaerner made no attempt to keep secret their intentions to eventually sell Cunard. Several key players including Royal Caribbean and P&O were known to have been approached – neither of which saw any real value in the company. So it caused somewhat of a stir when the Carnival Corporation took possession of Cunard Line on 3 April 1998. At the time Cunard's fleet

consisted of only five ships; *QE2*, *Vistafjord*, *Royal Viking Sun*, *Sea Goddess I* and *Sea Goddess II*. Carnival quickly set about reorganising the Cunard brand. *Vistafjord* was renamed *Caronia* and positioned with *QE2* to form the Cunard Line. *Royal Viking Sun* and the *Sea Goddesses* were moved to the Seabourn Brand and renamed *Seabourn Sun*, *Seabourn Goddess I* and *Seabourn Goddess II*. Both Cunard and Seabourn were operated under the direction of Larry Pimentel, Chairman and CEO of Cunard Line Ltd.

Carnival also made the unexpected move of announcing their intention to build a new ocean liner. This ship, planned at the time to be of similar dimensions to *QE2*, was codenamed Project *Queen Mary*. She would be the first transatlantic liner commissioned since *QE2*.

QE2 *at sea. (Authors' Collection)*

➤ *Caronia accommodation after the 1999 refurbishment. (Authors' Collection)*

➤➤ *The Caronia Restaurant as it appeared after the 1999 Bremerhaven refurbishment. (Authors' Collection)*

➤ *The Queens Room was also refurbished during the 1999 refit. (Authors' Collection)*

➤➤ *QE2 returned to service from her 1999 refit restored in traditional Cunard colours. (Cunard Line)*

Within the new Cunard brand, the *QE2* and *Caronia* were treated to refurbishments. These refits aimed to return the ships to their former glory, after months of patchy interior maintenance.

QE2's own refit cost £30 million and included the replacement or reupholstering of 3,500 pieces of furniture, new carpeting throughout the vessel, the replacement of wall coverings and curtains in public rooms

➤
QE2 looking somewhat awkward with her paint stripped. (Kenny Campbell)

➤➤
The sheer power of QE2 is seen when inspecting her variable pitch propellers. (Kenny Campbell)

➤
QE2's two bow thrusters produced 1,000hp per unit. (Kenny Campbell)

➤➤
A Lloyd Werft worker removes paint from QE2's hull. (Kenny Campbell)

Stripping paint from QE2 *during her 2004 refurbishment.* (Kenny Campbell)

Both aluminium and steel are clearly visible in this image from 2004. (Kenny Campbell)

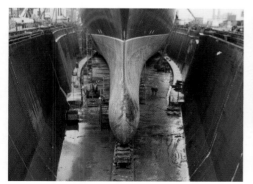

QE2's *bulbous bow.* (Kenny Campbell)

Looking forward under QE2. (Kenny Campbell)

QE2's *funnel towers above the Signal Deck. (Authors' Collection)*

and the redecoration of QE2's cabins and suites.

Three new luxury suites were also added. The Carinthia suite on Two Deck was created by enlarging the existing Mid-Ships Suite. The newly formed Aquitania suite, also on Two Deck, was built in the space formerly occupied by the hotel manager and cruise director's accommodation. On Boat Deck, the Radio Room (now obsolete) gave way to the wheelchair-friendly Caledonia suite.

The 1999 refit also saw QE2 return to her traditional colours of a matte-black hull with white superstructure, the speed stripe having been removed. This refit involved a complete hull-strip – right back to the bare metal. Caronia was also painted in traditional Cunard colours, giving the Cunard fleet a consistency not seen since QE2's launch.

'At 02:10 a.m. the rogue wave was sighted right ahead looming out of the darkness and it looked as though we were heading straight for the white cliffs of Dover. The wave seemed to take ages to reach us, but it was probably less than a minute before it broke with tremendous force over the bow of the QE2. An incredible shudder went through the ship followed a few moments later by two smaller shudders. At the same time the sea was cascading all over the fore part of the ship including the Bridge and it was several seconds before the water had drained away from the wheelhouse windows and the vision ahead was restored.'

Commodore Warwick – September 1995.

The newly refreshed Cunard fleet celebrated the arrival of the new Millennium positioned off Barbados. Aboard both ships there was much talk about the recently announced Project *Queen Mary*, which promised the construction of the first Cunard ocean liner since *QE2*.

In late 2001, *QE2*'s 1999 refit was complemented with a further US$12 million refit, which allowed for modifications to the Queens Grill and Queens Grill Lounge, both of which were treated to a new colour palette. The Yacht Club, Theatre, Mid-Ships Lobby and gym were refreshed, while the Queen Mary and Queen Elizabeth 'Grand Suites' were upgraded. Other work occurred behind the scenes, including a new sewage treatment plant and general maintenance on the propeller blades, bow thrusters and stabilisers.

New York was *QE2*'s second home, so it was fitting that she was the first passenger ship to return to the city after the September 11 attacks which had closed the port to passenger vessels. This triumphant return occurred on 8 January 2002, at the beginning of her annual world cruise.

QE2 *sails down the Solent bound for refit in Bremerhaven. (Cunard Line)*

Two years later *QE2* departed on her final world cruise as Cunard's flagship. *Queen Mary 2* had been placed into service in early 2004 and was due to take over as flagship from *QE2* at the culmination of her circumnavigation of the globe. The two Queens met for the first time in New York on 25 April – the first time two Cunard Queens had berthed in the city together since 1940 (when *Queen Mary* and *Queen Elizabeth* met there during the Second World War).

After a full day in the port, *QE2* and *QM2* undertook a tandem-crossing of the North Atlantic Ocean, a first in the company's long history. Upon arrival in Southampton on 1 May 2004, preparations were made for the symbolic handing over of the Boston Cup (presented to Samuel Cunard in 1840 by the people of its namesake) – which had been carried aboard *QE2* since she entered service.

Captain Ian McNaught of *QE2* and Commodore Ronald Warwick of *QM2* met near the G-Stairway by *QE2*'s Yacht Club where the cup was officially handed over, signalling the end of *QE2*'s reign as the Cunard flag carrier. Later that afternoon, *QE2* sailed from the Mayflower terminal bound for refit in Bremerhaven.

Did you know?
QE2 was the first ship
to sail more than 5
million nautical miles.

During her departure she passed the newly crowned *QM2* and the two liners exchanged whistles in celebration of the handover. Now, for the first time in *QE2*'s career, she would concentrate mainly on the British cruise market, leaving the vigour of the North Atlantic to her new sister.

Despite retiring as Cunard's primary Atlantic liner, QE2 still completed several crossings each year. These crossings formed part of her annual Autumn Colours voyage which saw her depart Southampton for a round-trip voyage via New York, Boston, Halifax (the birthplace of Samuel Cunard) and Quebec. QE2 also revisited the North Atlantic while re-positioning for her annual world cruise.

2007 marked the fortieth anniversary of QE2's launch, and a series of celebrations were organised by Cunard. One such event saw QE2 meet QM2 in Sydney Harbour – the first time since the Second World War that two Cunard Queens visited the famous harbour city together. This event was expected to draw a sizeable crowd, but no one could have anticipated

Australian's celebrate as QE2 meets QM2 in Sydney Harbour, February 2007. (Cunard Line)

Did you know?

When *QE2* was put into service she had no balcony cabins.

Looking into QE2 *at night was a thrill for passengers and visitors alike. (Authors' Collection)*

Did you know?

For most of her life, *QE2* was the most famous ship in service.

'My wife Judith and I were guests aboard *QE2* for her final North American (Canada-New England) voyage, September 10-30, 2008. As a native of Halifax, it was of particular interest to me to be present for the final calls to these historic maritime ports... particularly Boston, Saint John, Halifax and Quebec City. It was a wonderful trip, and for me a most appropriate way to make my final passage on this grand liner.'

John Langley – Chairman, Cunard Steamship Society.

just how many people this event would attract. Hundreds of thousands of people lined the banks of the harbour, bringing the city to a standstill. Although most people were impressed by *QM2*'s size, it was *QE2*'s arrival in the late afternoon that stole the show.

Crowds watch as QE2 *berths in Sydney Harbour in 2007. (Authors' Collection)*

QE2 *and* Norway *(ex-France) in close quarters at Bremerhaven. (Wolfhard Scheer)*

Ross Burnside was the last passenger to ever board QE2:

'Watching her slipping away down the river she was born on was an unforgettable and emotional experience. I persisted in contacting Cunard, never with much hope, but on the morning of Sunday 16th November the phone rang… I thought it was a mate having a laugh; it was Cunard returning my call. A cabin was available, was I interested? She was not convinced I could catch up with the ship. Neither was I, for flights were either fully booked, limited in schedule or comical in price. Malta on Tuesday, yes that would work!

One car, two planes, the London underground and a Southern train later, I arrived on the little island of Malta. The most ancient, ramshackled bus I had ever seen brought me to the centre of Valletta. It was hard to believe, almost surreal – there rising above the palm trees was her funnel. My heart was beating fast as I climbed the gangplank and stepped on board her for the first time in my life.

My all too short voyage is blurred in my memory…was it a dream: the passengers, the crew, the dining and the entertainment, her bow slicing through the open ocean, sun drenching her open decks, the reassuring deep sound from her funnel, the mesmerizing wash bubbling away to the horizon. My goodness she was alive!

I would have sailed again without question, but I left it too late for she is gone now. I will never forget how humbling it was to be carried along by her for a brief moment in time.'

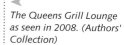
The Queens Grill Lounge as seen in 2008. (Authors' Collection)

Did you know?
QE2's kennels could accommodate up to eleven animals.

RETIREMENT

Despite *QE2*'s soaring popularity, her fortieth anniversary year was marred by sadness when, on 18 June 2007, Cunard announced plans for her retirement. The ship was sold for £50.5 million to Nakheel's Dubai World for use as a floating hotel at The Palm Jumeirah. Fortunately for *QE2*'s loyal following, there was still time to say a final farewell, with the official retirement date set for 27 November 2008.

QE2's fortieth anniversary celebrations peaked in September 2007 when she undertook a round-Britain voyage which took her from Southampton to Newcastle, Edinburgh, Greenock and Liverpool, before returning home.

At the end of 2007, *QE2* and *QM2* were joined in service by the new *Queen Victoria*. For the first time three Cunard Queens operated under the Cunard flag.

QE2's twenty-sixth and final world cruise offered a chance for the port-cities of the world to pay homage to the ship one final time. Highlights included a tandem-crossing with *Queen Victoria* which climaxed when, upon arrival in New York, the two ships were met by their larger sister, *QM2*. There were further rendezvous with *Queen Victoria* in Fort Lauderdale and Sydney, the latter visit causing a repeat of the festivities seen in 2007.

QE2 'crossed the line' for the final time as a Cunarder during this world cruise, en

route to Singapore from Fremantle. Upon arrival in Southampton in April 2008, she was met again by *Queen Victoria* and *QM2* for the last ever meeting of the three Queens.

After *QE2*'s retirement was announced, Cunard reorganised the final months of her schedule to allow for a series of farewell cruises. These included a 'Farewell Britain' cruise which re-traced her fortieth anniversary voyage (with the addition of Cóbh in Ireland). She also undertook two transatlantic crossings in tandem with *QM2*, during which *QE2* bid an emotional farewell to New York and America.

Upon arrival back in Southampton, the ship took two regular cruises during which the synagogue was carefully removed from the location it had occupied on Three Deck for nearly forty years.

QE2's final voyage had an inauspicious start when, on the morning of 11 November 2008, the ship briefly ran aground on a sandbank in the Solent on her final approach to Southampton. Five tugs were required to assist in pulling the ship free and she arrived at her berth one hour late.

Once docked, divers were sent to inspect the hull for possible damage, while on-board the crew were preparing for a farewell visit from HRH The Duke of Edinburgh. Prince Phillip was taken on a tour of *QE2* led by

One million poppies are dropped to mark Remembrance Day. (Andy Fitzsimmons)

➤
Bi-planes drop one million poppies over QE2. (Andy Fitzsimmons)

➤➤
Southampton celebrates the life of QE2 with a magnificent fireworks display. (Andy Fitzsimmons)

Commodore John Burton Hall (retired) and Captain Ian McNaught. After visiting the Bridge, Engine Control Room and various public rooms, the official party moved onto the Upper Deck (just aft of the Yacht Club) for a one minute silence in honour of Remembrance Day. Afterwards, one million poppies were dropped over QE2's open decks before a RAF Harrier Jump-Jet performed an aerobatics display over the ship.

That evening the ropes were slipped from Southampton's wharf for the last time as QE2 gracefully sailed towards the turning ground in the port. There, a spectacular fireworks display celebrating the ship's connection to the city was watched by passengers, crew and the people of Southampton. Finally, QE2 sailed away from her home, never to return again.

The ship's final voyage was described by those on-board as being 'like any other voyage', with the crew maintaining the utmost professionalism until the very end. It was not until the final twenty-four hours that the real sense of impending loss hit those on-board, including Commodore Ronald Warwick (retired), who had been

An Emirates Airbus A380 pays tribute to QE2 as she arrives in Dubai. (Cunard Line)

Did you know?

QE2 was more than four-and-a-half-times longer than Cunard's first ship, RMS *Britannia*.

Fireworks as New York celebrates the three Cunard Queens. (Cunard Line)

*More fireworks for QE2
in Dubai. (Cunard Line)*

QE2's 2008 World Cruise was a farewell celebration. (Authors' Collection)

QE2 sails into the sunset on her final Australian departure. (Authors' Collection)

Did you know?
QE2 crossed the Atlantic 806 times.

appointed by Nahkeel to be QE2's master once she arrived in Dubai.

26 November 2008 was a spectacularly sunny day in Dubai. Hundreds of small boats were gathered near The World Islands off the coast of Dubai to meet QE2 and welcome her to her new home. The Royal Yacht Dubai escorted QE2 towards the harbour while the crew of the British Royal Naval vessel HMS Lancaster honoured the ship with three cheers.

Upon docking in Dubai, QE2's career with Cunard came to an end. On 27 November, after the passengers had departed the ship, a small ceremony took place on QE2's port Bridge Wing where Carol Marlow, President of Cunard Line, officially handed the ship over to His Highness Sheikh Mohammed bin Rashid Al Maktoum, Vice President and Prime Minister of the UAE and ruler of

The Cunard flag flies aboard QE2. *(Authors' Collection)*

Entering Port Mina Rashid at the culmination of her final voyage. (Ross Burnside)

QE2 *was born on the River Clyde. (Ross Burnside)*

Dubai. Shortly afterwards, the distinctive Golden Lion was lowered from *QE2*'s mast for the last time, to be replaced by the flag of Nahkeel, while the Union Jack was replaced by the flag of the United Arab Emirates.

With her arrival in Dubai, *QE2*'s ocean-going story ended. However, her new life

◄ ▲
The final sunset for Cunard's QE2 – 26 November 2008. (Ross Burnside)

▲
The QE2 at rest in Dubai. (Ross Burnside)

◄
The magnificent QE2 alongside in Malta on her final voyage. (Ross Burnside)

as a floating hotel has only just begun. It is the hope of many that her new career will preserve what is special about *QE2*, allowing further generations to have the opportunity to enjoy this great ship.

Captain Ian McNaught remembers taking command of QE2 *for the first time:*

'For me it was a boyhood ambition realised, and as the other Captain goes home on leave, you suddenly realise that a crew of 1,000 are all there to help you, but you can feel very much on your own. However, when you stand on the Bridge Wing to leave port, you know inside yourself that this is probably the biggest day of your life and that everything you have ever learned really counts. You feel very proud and a little nervous at the same time, but love every minute of it as you give the order, "Let go fore and aft, and let's go to sea gentlemen".'

QE2 *had a 39ft paying-off-pennant; 1ft for every year of service. (Ross Burnside)*

QE2 SPECIFICATIONS

General information (while with Cunard)

Name:	Queen Elizabeth 2 (QE2)
Gross registered tonnage (1969):	65,863 tons.
Gross registered tonnage (2008):	70,327 tons.
Length:	963ft.
Width:	105.25ft.
Builders:	John Brown Shipyard / Upper Clyde Shipbuilders.
Keel laid:	5 July 1965.
Launched:	20 September 1967 by HM Queen Elizabeth II.
Maiden voyage:	Departed 2 May 1969.
Final voyage:	Departed 11 November 2008.
Maximum passenger capacity (2008):	1,777 persons.
Standard crew capacity:	1,040 persons.
Port of registry (1969-2008):	Southampton, England.
Official number:	336703.
Official signal letters:	G.B.T.T.

Engine information (1967–1986)

Engines: 2 x double reduction geared turbines.

Boilers: 3 x high-pressure water tube boilers, of 278 tons each.

Propellers: 2 six-bladed fixed pitch propellers.

Output at propellers: 110,000 shaft horsepower.

Engine information (1987–2008)

Diesel engines: 9 x 9 cylinder MAN B&W Diesels.

Electric motors: 2 x GEC, one on each propeller shaft.

Boilers: 9 x exhaust gas, 2 x oil fired.

Propellers: 2 x five-bladed outward turning LIPS-controllable pitch propellers.

Output at propellers: 44mw each.

Fuel consumption: 18.05 tons per hour (433 tons per day) for all nine engines.

115

Bow thrusters:	2 x Stone Kamewa, 1,000 horsepower each.
Stabilizers:	4 x Denny Brown.
Rudder weight:	75 tons.
Forward anchors:	2 x 12.5 tons.
Forward anchor cables:	2 x 1,080ft long.
Aft anchor:	1 x 7.25 tons.
Aft anchor cables:	1 x 720ft long.
Service speed:	28.5 knots.
Top cruising speed:	32.5 knots.

QE2 MILESTONES (WITH CUNARD)

9 September 1964: Shipyards are invited to tender for the construction of Q4.

30 November 1964: All bids for the building of Q4 are returned to Cunard.

30 December 1964: Building contract signed by Sir John Brocklebank (Cunard) and Lord Aberconway (John Brown) for the building of Q4 (736).

5 July 1965: *QE2*'s keel is successfully laid at John Brown Shipyard.

20 September 1967: *QE2* is launched by HM Queen Elizabeth II.

19 November 1968: HRH Prince Charles is *QE2*'s first passenger on the short voyage to Greenock. He has the privilege of sounding the liner's whistle.

26 November 1968: *QE2* begins her preliminary sea trials. She achieves 164rpm.

30 November 1968: Trials of *QE2* end unexpectedly when fuel oil contaminates her steam propulsion system. She returns to Greenock for repairs.

18 December 1968: Second technical trials begin. *QE2* achieves 177rpm.

23rd December 1968: *QE2*'s acceptance sea trials commence.

24-28 December 1968: Pressure gauge piping fractures cause vibrations in the starboard engine. Port engine begins to show signs of malfunction.

25 March 1969: *QE2* commences builder's technical trials.

27 March 1969: *QE2*'s trials are completed.

30 March 1969: The liner commences her shakedown cruise.

7 April 1969: *QE2* arrives back in Southampton.

18 April 1969: Cunard take possession of their new flagship.

22 April 1969: *QE2* commences her 'mini-maiden voyage' to the Canary Islands.

30th April, 1969: *QE2* arrives home following her 'mini-maiden voyage'.

1 May 1969: HM Queen Elizabeth II and HRH the Duke of Edinburgh visit *QE2*.

2 May 1969: *QE2* departs on her maiden voyage fifteen minutes late.

7 May 1969: *QE2* arrives in New York for the first time.

29 May 1969: HRH the Duke of Edinburgh visits the ship to present awards on behalf of the Council of Industrial Design.

8 January 1971: *QE2* goes to the rescue of the French liner *Antilles*.

25 August 1971: Cunard Line's final independent board meeting. The Trafalgar House Co. takes control of Cunard Line the following day.

17 May 1972: Captain William Law receives a coded message from Cunard of a possible bomb aboard *QE2*.

18 May 1972: A bomb disposal team parachute into the sea and are brought aboard *QE2* for inspection. No bomb is found.

21 June 1972: Joseph Lindisi is arrested and charged with attempted extortion against *QE2* (and American Airlines). He is sentenced to twenty years in gaol.

October 1972: First penthouse suites are added to *QE2* during her refit in Southampton.

10 January 1975: *QE2* departs New York on her first world cruise.

25 March 1975: *QE2* transits the Panama Canal for the first time, making it the largest passenger ship to travel through the canal at the time.

3 December 1977: *QE2* begins refurbishment in New Jersey where the Queen Elizabeth and Queen Mary suites are added. This refit forms the only US contribution to *QE2*'s external structure.

3 May 1982: *QE2* is requisitioned for use by the British Government as a troopship in the Falklands Islands campaign.

4 May 1982: *QE2* arrives in Southampton and is registered as 'STUFT' (Ship Taken Up From Trade).

5 May 1982: *QE2*'s war service conversion begins.

12 May 1982: *QE2*'s war service conversion is completed. 3,000 troops (5th Infantry Brigade) embark on the *QE2*, bound for the Falklands.

27 May 1982: *QE2* arrives in Cumberland Bay, Central South Georgia.

28 May 1982: Troop transfer from *QE2* begins.

11 June 1982: *QE2* arrives home and is greeted by HM The Queen Mother aboard the Royal Yacht *Britannia.*

12 June 1982: *QE2* begins extensive post-war refit at King George V Dry-Dock in Southampton.

15 August 1982: *QE2* returns to service sporting a pebble grey hull and traditional Cunard funnel colours.

20 October 1986: *QE2* makes her last transatlantic crossing as a steamship.

27 October 1986: Arrives in Bremerhaven, Germany, for refitting and conversion to a diesel-powered ship.

20 February 1987: *QE2* is given her new, wider funnel.

25 April 1987: Handover ceremony occurs in which the diesel-powered *QE2* is returned to Cunard Line.

28 April 1987: The diesel-powered *QE2* arrives in Southampton for the first time.

29 April 1987: HRH Princess Diana visits *QE2*.

29 April 1987: *QE2* begins first transatlantic crossing as a diesel ship.

23 July 1988: The ship returns to Lloyd Werft in Bremerhaven to have new propellers fitted.

27 March 1989: *QE2* begins charter to a Japanese consortium for a seventy-two-day celebration of the 130th anniversary of Yokohama.

17 July 1990: *QE2* completes fastest ever eastbound crossing in four days, six hours and fifty-seven minutes.

24 July 1990: *QE2* arrives in Liverpool for the first time where she is met by an estimated one million spectators.

26 July 1990: Captain R.W. Warwick is appointed master of *QE2*, the first time in Cunard's history that a son has commanded the same ship as his father.

27 July 1990: HM Queen Elizabeth II (aboard *QE2*) becomes the first reigning monarch to sail on a commercial liner with passengers.

7 August 1992: *QE2* runs aground off the coast of Martha's Vineyard. After re-floating, she proceeds to Boston for temporary repairs.

1 September 1992: *QE2* departs Boston for Blohm + Voss, Hamburg, for permanent repairs.

20 November 1994: *QE2* arrives at Blohm + Voss to begin her 'Project Lifestyle' refurbishment.

17 December 1994: *QE2* sails into the headlines when she departs for New York with men on-board still working on the refurbishment.

14 June 1995: *QE2* departs New York bound for Southampton on her 1,000th voyage.

11 September 1995: *QE2* encounters a 95ft rogue wave caused by Hurricane Luis.

4 March 1996: The Trafalgar House Co. (and thus Cunard) is sold to Kvaerner.

22 November 1996: *QE2* undergoes further refurbishment in Southampton in preparation for 1997 SOLAS requirements.

29-31 March 1998: South African President Nelson Mandela sails from Durban to Cape Town on-board *QE2*.

3 April 1998: Cunard Line is sold to Carnival Corporation.

12 December 1999: *QE2* returns to service after her £30 million refit.

31 December 1999: *QE2* ends the twentieth century positioned off Barbados alongside fleet mate *Caronia*.

20 November 2001: *QE2* departs Southampton for a refit at Lloyd Werft in Bremerhaven.

26 April 2002: *QE2* transports an original whistle from RMS *Queen Mary* which is destined to be used aboard the new *QM2*.

29 August 2002: *QE2* completes 5 million nautical miles, setting a new world record.

25 April 2004: *QE2* meets her new sister *QM2* for the first time in New York after completing her last westbound transatlantic crossing as Cunard's flagship.

25 April 2004: *QE2* departs on her first tandem eastbound transatlantic crossing with *QM2*.

1 May 2004: *QE2*'s reign as flagship ends. She is recognised as Cunard's longest-serving flagship. She heads to Bremerhaven for refit.

4 September 2005: *QE2* becomes the longest-serving Cunard ship in the company's history.

24 April 2006: *QE2* begins a sixteen-day refurbishment at Lloyd Werft, Bremerhaven.

18 June 2007: *QE2*'s retirement and sale to Nahkeel is announced.

20 September 2007: *QE2*'s forty-year anniversary. As part of the celebrations she returns to her birthplace on the Clyde.

11 November 2008: *QE2* departs Southampton for the last time, bound for Dubai.

26 November 2008: *QE2* arrives in Dubai. She is escorted by the Royal Yacht *Dubai* and HMS *Lancaster* to Port Rashid.

27 November 2008: The last passengers disembark. Nahkeel takes possession of *QE2*. The Cunard flag is lowered for the last time and Captain Ian McNaught is presented with *QE2*'s 39ft-long paying-off pennant.

GLOSSARY OF NAUTICAL (AND *QE2*) TERMS

Abeam	Off the side of the ship, at a 90° angle to its length.
Aft	Near or towards the back of the ship.
Amidships	Towards the middle of the ship.
Bow	The forwardmost part of a vessel.
Bridge	Navigational command centre of the ship.
Colours	The national flag or emblem flown by the ship.
Draft	Depth of water measured from the surface of the water to the ship's keel.
Forward	Near or towards the front of the ship.
Heritage Trail	A self-guided tour aboard *QE2* that visits objects of historic value.
Hove to	When the ship is in open sea and not moving.
Hull	The body of the vessel that stretches from the keel to the superstructure (*QE2*'s is painted black).
Keel	The 'spine' of the ship, to which the hull frames are attached. The lowest point of a vessel.
Knot	One nautical mile per hour (one nautical mile = 1,852 metres or 1.15 statute miles).
Leeward	The direction in which the wind blows, or the sheltered side.
Pitch	The alternate rise and fall of the ship, evident when at sea.
Port	The left side of the ship when facing forward.

SOLAS	Safety Of Life At Sea regulations that govern shipboard safety requirements.
Starboard	The right side of the ship when facing forward.
Stern	The rearmost part of a vessel.
Superstructure	The body of the ship above the main deck or hull (*QE2*'s is painted white).
Tender	A small vessel (sometimes a lifeboat) used to transport passengers from ship to shore.
Wake	The trail of disturbed water left behind the ship when it is moving.
Windward	The direction from which the wind is blowing.

BIBLIOGRAPHY

BOOKS:

Baynard, F.O. and Miller, W.H. (1991), *Picture History of the Cunard Line, 1840-1990* (Dover Publications, United Kingdom).

Bombail, M., Buchanan, G., Cousteau, J., Duffy, J., Hare, S., Verlomme, H. (2000), *A Tribute to QE2 and the North Atlantic Ocean* (Rouge de Mars, Switzerland).

Buchanan, G. (1996), *Queen Elizabeth 2, Sailing into the New Millennium* (Past and Present Publishing, United Kingdom).

Dawson, P. (2005), *The Liner,* Conway (Marine Press, United Kingdom).

Dawson, P. (2000), *Cruise Ships, An Evolution in Design,* Conway (Marine Press, United Kingdom).

Grant, R.,G. (2007), *Flight: The Complete History* (Dorling Kindersley Limited, United Kingdom).

Harding, S. (1995), *Gray Ghost: The RMS Queen Mary at War* (3rd ed.) (Pictorial Histories Publishing Co., USA).

Harvey, C. and Cartwright, R. (2006), *The Saga Sisters* (The History Press, Tempus Imprint, United Kingdom).

Hutchings, D. (2002), *QE2 – A Ship for all Seasons* (Waterfront, United Kingdom).

Hutchings, D. (1990), *RMS Queen Elizabeth: From Victory to Valhalla* (Kingfisher Publications, United Kingdom).

Miller, W.H. (2008), *The QE2 – A Picture History* (Dover Publications, United Kingdom).

Miller, W.H. (2001), *Picture History of British Ocean Liners, 1900 to Present* (Dover Publications, United Kingdom).

Miller, W.H. and Correia, L.M. (1999), *RMS Queen Elizabeth 2 of 1969* (Liner Books, Portugal).

Miller, W.H. (1995), *Pictorial Encyclopedia of Ocean Liners, 1860 to 1994* (Constable and Co., United Kingdom).

Peter, B., Dawson, P., and Johnston, I. (2008), *QE2: Britain's Greatest Liner* (Ferry Publications, United Kingdom).

Plowman, P. (2007), *Australian Cruise Ships* (Rosenberg Publishing PTY, LTD, Australia).

Storey, T. (2007), *QE2: Farewell Queen of the Seas (40th Anniversary Tribute)* (Trinity Mirror Sport Media, United Kingdom).

Thatcher, C. (2007), *QE2: Forty Years Famous* (Simon & Schuster Ltd, United Kingdom).

Warwick, R.W. (1999), *QE2 – The Cunard Line Flagship, Queen Elizabeth 2* (3rd ed.) (Norton, United Kingdom).

Williams, D. (2004), *Cunard's Legendary Queens of the Seas* (Ian Allan Publishing, United Kingdom).

Williams, D. and Forty, J. (2001), *Ocean Liners* (PRC Publishing Limited, United Kingdom).

WEBSITES:

Chris' Cunard Page: http://www.chriscunard.com

Chris' *QE2* Pages: http://www.chriscunard.com/qe2.htm

Cunard Line UK Website: http://www.cunard.co.uk

Sam Warwick's *QE2* Website: http://www.qe2.org.uk

CONVERSATIONS / INTERVIEWS:

Commodore R.W. Warwick – Personal Conversations
Captain I. McNaught – Personal Conversations
Chief Engineer P. Yeoman – Personal Conversations
Commodore J. Burton-Hall – Personal Correspondence
Michael Gallagher, Cunard Line – Personal Correspondence

<u>For Further Reading</u>:

About QE2: *QE2: A Photographic Journey* by Chris Frame and Rachelle Cross – www.qe2book.com

About QM2: *QM2: A Photographic Journey* by Chris Frame and Rachelle Cross – www.qm2book.com

About Queen Victoria: *Queen Victoria: A Photographic Journey* by Chris Frame and Rachelle Cross – www.queenvictoriabook.com